SCOTTISH COOKING

RECIPES FROM SCOTLAND

Sue McDougall

DOMINO BOOKS (WALES) LTD

METRIC/IMPERIAL/AMERICAN UNITS

We are all used to doubling or halving a recipe. Thus, a Victoria sandwich may be made using 4 oz each of flour, sugar and butter with 2 eggs or 6 oz each of flour, sugar and butter with 3 eggs. The proportions of the ingredients are unchanged. This must be so for all units. Use either the metric units or the imperial units given in the recipes, do not mix the two.

It is not practical to give the exact equivalents of metric and imperial units because 1 oz equals 28.35 g and 1 pint equals 568 ml. The tables on page vi indicate suitable quantities but liquids should be carefully added to obtain the correct consistency. See also the charts on page iv.

PINTS TO MILLILITRES AND LITRES

The following are approximations only

$\frac{1}{4}$ pint = 150 ml

$\frac{1}{2}$ pint = 275 ml

$\frac{3}{4}$ pint = 425 ml

1 pint = 575 ml

$1\frac{3}{4}$ pints = 1000 ml (1 litre)

3 pints = $1\frac{1}{2}$ litres

© D C P and E J P, 1997
7th reprint 2004
Domino Books (Wales) Ltd
P O Box 32
Swansea SA1 1FN
UK
Tel. 01792 459378
Fax. 01792 466337
email: sales@dominobooks.co.uk
www.dominobooks.co.uk

CONTENTS

iv   The following charts give the approximate equivalents for metric and imperial weights, and oven temperatures.

Ounces	Approx g to nearest whole number	Approx g to nearest whole 25 g
1	28	25
2	57	50
3	85	75
4	113	125
5	142	150
6	170	175
7	198	200
8	226	225
9	255	250
10	283	275
11	311	300
12	340	350
13	368	375
14	396	400
15	428	425
16	456	450

OVEN TEMPERATURE GUIDE

	Electricity °C	°F	Gas Mark
Very cool	110	225	$\frac{1}{4}$
	130	250	$\frac{1}{2}$
Cool	140	275	1
	150	300	2
Moderate	170	325	3
	180	350	4
Moderately hot	190	375	5
	200	400	6
Hot	220	425	7
	230	450	8
Very hot	240	475	9

When using this chart for weights over 16 ounces, add the appropriate figures in the column giving the nearest whole number of grammes and then adjust to the nearest unit of 25. For example, 18 oz (16 oz + 2 oz) becomes 456 + 57 = 513 to the nearest whole number and 500 g to the nearest unit of 25.

Throughout the book, 1 teaspoon = 5 ml and 1 tablespoon = 15 ml.

FOREWORD

You don't have to be Scottish to enjoy the wonderful flavour of the country's cooking. Much is robust, warm, the kind of food needed by people used to working hard in weather that is not always kind. Much is delicate, unique flavours appreciated by sensitive palates.

Scottish meat such as beef from the Aberdeen Angus, Galloway or Highland Shorthorn has an international reputation for quality. Sheep are well suited to life on the slopes of Scottish mountains. The Black-faced breed grazes on heather which gives its meat its own special flavour while the Shetland breed yields meat with a slightly gamey taste. Some of the best pork and bacon comes from Aberdeenshire, the north-east and Ayrshire. Feasting is part of the Scottish tradition, especially Hogmanay (New Year's Eve celebrations) and Burn's Night (25 January). Haggis, essential on Burn's Night, is probably the best known Scottish meat dish.

Scotland is famous for the game which inhabits the moors and forests. Roe and fallow deer, and the more common red deer, are found wild throughout the Highlands. Some 90% is exported but there is still plenty for the home market and much is used in sausages, pâtés and fresh, smoked joints. Wild deer are in season from July to the end of February but venison from deer farms is available all the year.

With so much coastline, fishing is an important part of Scotland's economy and fish is an important food. Herrings are especially tasty (try them coated with oatmeal and fried crisp and brown) while Loch Fyne Kippers are regarded as the best in the world. The coast around Fife and the Western Isles is famous for shellfish - lobsters, crabs, scallops and winkles. Freshwater fish come from the pure water of the deep locks and fast-flowing rivers. Try grilled trout stuffed with soft cheese and coated with almonds, Arbroath smokies, Finnan haddock and, of course, smoked salmon.

Scotland produces two-thirds of the UK's raspberries. Much of the fruit is made into jams and conserves but the taste of the fresh fruit is a treat not to be missed.

Oatmeal is often used in Scottish cooking: oatcakes, oatmeal bannocks, oatmeal bread, oatmeal scones, cream crowdie ... The basic recipe for Scottish shortbread uses butter, caster sugar and flour. This is eaten all year round but it is particularly popular at New Year.

The national drink of Scotland, whisky, is used in many recipes. So also is Drambuie, a whisky-based liqueur said to be made from a secret recipe of Bonnie Prince Charlie. Drinking this is sipping Scottish history.

Some of the recipes are in this book, others are in the companion books, *Scottish Teas, Customs and Cooking from Scotland* and *Celtic Recipes*. I hope you enjoy making these dishes and sharing them with your family and friends.

S.M.

AMERICAN MEASURES

American measures are given by volume and weight using standard cups and spoons.

US Standard Measuring Spoons and Cups

1 tablespoon = 3 teaspoons = $\frac{1}{2}$ fluid ounce = 14•2 ml

2 tablespoons = 1 fluid ounce = 28 ml

4 tablespoons = $\frac{1}{4}$ cup

5 tablespoons = $\frac{1}{3}$ cup

8 tablespoons = $\frac{1}{2}$ cup

10 tablespoons = $\frac{2}{3}$ cup

12 tablespoons = $\frac{3}{4}$ cup

16 tablespoons = 1 cup = 8 fluid ounces = $\frac{1}{2}$ US pint

32 tablespoons = 2 cups = 16 fluid ounces = 1 US pint.

Metric (Imperial)	American
1 teaspoon	1 teaspoon
1 tablespoon	1 tablespoon
$1\frac{1}{2}$ tablespoons	2 tablespoons
2 tablespoons	3 tablespoons
3 tablespoons	$\frac{1}{4}$ (scant) cup
4 tablespoons	5 tablespoons
5 tablespoons	6 tablespoons
$5\frac{1}{2}$ tablespoons	7 tablespoons
6 tablespoons (scant $\frac{1}{4}$ pint)	$\frac{1}{2}$ cup
$\frac{1}{4}$ pint	$\frac{2}{3}$ cup
scant $\frac{1}{2}$ pint	1 cup
$\frac{1}{2}$ pint (10 fl oz)	$1\frac{1}{4}$ cups
$\frac{3}{4}$ pint (15 fl oz)	scant 2 cups
$\frac{4}{5}$ pint (16 fl oz)	2 cups (1 pint)
1 pint (20 fl oz)	$2\frac{1}{2}$ cups

Metric (Imperial)	American
flour, plain or self-raising	
15 g ($\frac{1}{2}$ oz)	2 tablespoons
25 g (1oz)	$1\frac{1}{4}$ cups
100/125 g (4 oz)	1 cup
sugar, caster or granulated, brown (firmly packed)	
25 g (1 oz)	2 tablespoons
100/125 g (4 oz)	$\frac{1}{2}$ cup
200/225 g (8 oz)	1 cup
butter, margarine, fat	
1 oz	2 tablespoons
225 g (8 oz)	1 cup
150 g (5 oz) shredded suet	1 cup

1 cup (American) contains approximately

100/125 g (4 oz) grated cheese, 50 g (2 oz) fresh breadcrumbs,
100 g (4 oz) dried breadcrumbs,
100/125 g (4 oz) pickled beetroot, button mushrooms, shelled
peas, red/blackcurrants, 5 oz strawberries,
175 g (6 oz) raisins, currants, sultanas, chopped candied peel,
stoned dates,
225 g (8 oz) glace cherries, 150 g (5 oz) shelled whole walnuts,
100 g (4 oz) chopped nuts,
75 g (3 oz) desiccated coconut,
225 g (8 oz) cottage cheese,
100/125 g (4 oz) curry powder,
225 g (8 oz) minced raw meat,
$\frac{3}{8}$ pint ($7\frac{1}{2}$ fl oz) cream.

SOUPS

PARTAN BREE

METRIC

1 crab
75 g rice
500 ml milk
500 ml white stock
$\frac{1}{2}$ teaspoon anchovy essence
125 ml single cream
salt and pepper

IMPERIAL

1 crab
3 oz rice
1 pint milk
1 pint white stock
$\frac{1}{2}$ teaspoon anchovy essence
$\frac{1}{4}$ pint single cream
salt and pepper.

Leave the crab in cold water for 20 minutes. Plunge quickly into salted water and boil the crab for 25 minutes. Allow to cool in the water. Remove the claws and take out the flesh from the large claws. Remove the apron, break up and remove the white flesh. Discard the grey gills. Remove the flesh from the shell. Rinse the rice in cold water, strain and add to the milk in a saucepan. Add a pinch of salt. Bring the rice and milk to the boil. Cover and simmer gently until the rice is soft. Stir in the the crab meat. Sieve the mixture (or use a liquidiser). Return the liquidised fish mixture to the saucepan and stir in the stock. Bring to the boil, stirring all the time. Remove the soup from the heat. Add the anchovy essence and stir in the cream. Keep hot but do not allow to boil again. Serve hot.

CULLEN SKINK

METRIC
1 Finnan-haddie
1 small onion
1 medium sized potato
25 g butter
500 ml milk
salt and pepper

IMPERIAL
1 Finnan-haddie
1 small onion
1 medium sized potato
1 oz butter
1 pint milk
salt and pepper

Skin and wash the fish. Place in a pan or saucepan and cover with water. Skin and slice the onion. Add to the fish. Season and simmer gently until the fish is cooked. Remove the flesh of the fish and flake. Return the fish bones to the stock in the pan and cook slowly for about an hour. Peel and boil the potato in salted water. Drain. Mash with the butter. Strain the fish stock and add the milk and flaked fish. Thicken with a little of the potato.

SCOTCH BROTH

METRIC
neck of mutton or lean stewing beef
15 g pearl barley
carrots
small turnip
parsnip
medium-sized onion
50 g shelled or frozen peas
1•5 litres water
4 tablespoons chopped kail
salt and pepper

IMPERIAL
neck of mutton or lean stewing beef
$\frac{1}{2}$ oz pearl barley
carrots
small turnip
parsnip
medium-sized onion
2 oz shelled or frozen peas
3 pints water
4 tablespoons chopped kail
salt and pepper

Cut up the meat and remove as much fat as possible. Wash the barley. Place the meat, and any bones, with the barley in a large saucepan. Cover with water and bring to the boil. Skim. Peel and dice the carrots, turnip and parsnip. Skin and slice the onion. Add all the vegetables, except the kail, to the saucepan. Season to taste and simmer for 4 hours. Remove any fat from the surface and add the chopped kail. Cook for 10 minutes. Serve hot.

COCK A LEEKIE

METRIC	*IMPERIAL*
10 prunes (optional)	*10 prunes (optional)*
2 kg boiling fowl	*4-5 lb boiling fowl*
giblets	*giblets*
3 rashers bacon	*3 rashers bacon*
8 leeks	*8 leeks*
2 litres water	*4 pints water*
pinch of parsley	*pinch of parsley*
pinch of thyme	*pinch of thyme*
1 bay leaf	*1 bay leaf*
salt and pepper	*salt and pepper*

If prunes are used soak them overnight. Clean the bird and place in a large saucepan. Wash the giblets and cut up the bacon. Add to the pan. Wash the leeks and discard the coarser outer leaves. Cut the leeks into small pieces and add to the pan. Pour in water to just cover the bird and season. Bring to the boil and skim. Season with the herbs, salt and pepper. Cover and simmer for $3\frac{1}{2}$ hours until the bird is tender. Stone and halve the prunes if used. Add to the soup. Simmer for a further 30 minutes. Remove the bird and giblets and cut into large pieces. Place in individual soup bowls. Pour the soup over the bird and garnish with parsley.

GROUSE SOUP

METRIC
Stock:
marrowbone
1•5 litres water
3 rashers streaky bacon
2 sticks celery
6 black peppercorns
pinch cayenne pepper
salt and pepper
Soup:
pair grouse
25 g bacon fat
15 g seasoned butter
butter for frying
50 g coarse oatmeal
1 tablespoon cream or
1 tablespoon red wine and
1 teaspoon whisky
salt and pepper

IMPERIAL
Stock:
marrowbone
3 pints water
3 rashers streaky bacon
2 sticks celery
6 black peppercorns
pinch cayenne pepper
salt and pepper
Soup:
pair grouse
1 oz bacon fat
$\frac{1}{2}$ oz seasoned butter
butter for frying
2 oz coarse oatmeal
1 tablespoon cream or
1 tablespoon red wine and
1 teaspoon whisky
salt and pepper

Stock: Clean the bone. Put in a pan and cover with water. Cut up the bacon and add to the water. Clean and break up the celery and add to the pan. Season and bring to the boil. Skim well. Simmer for 2 hours then strain into a large saucepan or casserole.

Soup: Clean and pluck the birds. Coat the breasts with bacon fat and put a nub of seasoned butter inside each. Cook for 30 minutes in a moderately hot oven (190°C, 375°F, gas mark 5). Remove all the meat from the birds and mince

- except the breasts. Melt the butter in a pan and fry the oatmeal until lightly brown. Stir in the stock and add the minced meat. Simmer for 20 minutes. Dice the breasts and lightly fry in butter. Add to the soup. Remove from the heat and add the cream or wine and whisky.

TATTIE DROOTLE

METRIC	IMPERIAL
1 large onion	*1 1arge onion*
1 1arge leek	*1 large leek*
25 g butter	*1 oz butter*
400 g potatoes	*1 1b potatoes*
1 litre stock	*2 pints stock*
1 tablespoon single cream	*1 tablespoon single cream*
1 tablespoon chopped parsley	*1 tablespoon chopped parsley*
salt and pepper	*salt and pepper*

Skin the onion. Discard the outer leaves of the leek. Cut up the onion and leek and fry in the fat until soft but not discoloured. Peel the potatoes and add to the stock. Add the onion and leek. Season. Simmer gently for $1\frac{1}{2}$ hours. Remove from the heat and stir in the cream. Re-heat but do not allow the soup to boil again. Serve hot garnished with parsley. NB. If a pressure cooker is used boil at 15 lb pressure for 10 minutes. Cool, liquidise and add the cream. Re-heat but do not allow the soup to boil again.

FISH

SOUSED HERRING

METRIC	IMPERIAL
1 small onion	*1 small onion*
4 herrings	*4 herrings*
1 bay leaf	*1 bay leaf*
125 ml vinegar	$\frac{1}{4}$ *pint vinegar*
125 ml water	$\frac{1}{4}$ *pint water*
1 blade mace	*1 blade rnace*
10 black peppercorns	*10 black peppercorns*
$\frac{1}{4}$ *teaspoon salt*	$\frac{1}{4}$ *teaspoon salt*
few green and red cocktail onions	*few green and red cocktail onions*

Skin and cut the onions into rings. Clean and scale the fish. Split each herring along the underside. Open and ease out the backbone and as many small bones as possible. Wash and dry. Season and place a small piece of bayleaf and onion ring on each fish. Roll up from head to tail with the skin outside and secure with a cocktail stick. Place in an ovenproof dish. Cover with the vinegar and water and add the spices. Bake in the centre of a moderate oven (180°C, 350°F, gas mark 4) for 45 minutes. When cold, serve in the liquid garnished with green and red cocktail onions.

HAM AND HADDIE

METRIC	IMPERIAL
1 smoked Moray Firth haddock	*1 smoked Moray Firth haddock*
25 g butter	*1 oz butter*
2 slices smoked ham	*2 slices smoked ham*
pepper	*pepper*

Place the haddock in a pan and cover with water. Simmer for 2 minutes. Turn the fish and simmer for a further 2 minutes. Take out the fish and remove the skin and bones. Melt the butter in a frying pan and place the ham slices in the pan. Turn ham once then place the fish on top. Season with pepper. Cover and heat gently for 2-3 minutes.

POACHED BURN TROUT

METRIC	IMPERIAL
Fish	*Fish*
4 trout	*4 trout*
Court bouillon	***Court bouillon***
1 litre water	*2 pints water*
1 tablespoon lemon juice	*1 tablespoon lemon juice*
1 teaspoon salt	*1 teaspoon salt*
$\frac{1}{2}$ bay leaf	*$\frac{1}{2}$ bay leaf*
1 sprig parsley	*1 sprig parsley*
1 small piece blade mace	*1 small piece blade mace*
6 peppercorns	*6 peppercorns*
2 teaspoons diced onion	*2 teaspoons diced onion*
2 teaspoons diced carrot	*2 teaspoons diced carrot*
2 tablespoons tarragon vinegar	*2 tablespoons tarragon vinegar*
2 tablespoons white wine	*2 tablespoons white wine*

Court bouillon Boil all the ingredients for the court bouillon in an enamel saucepan and simmer for 20 minutes. Strain.

Fish Clean the fish and place in a shallow dish. Cover with the court bouillon and simmer for 10 -15 minutes. Serve with potatoes baked in their jackets and mixed salad.

TROUT IN OATMEAL

METRIC
trout
large nub of butter per fish
10 g coarse oatmeal per fish
parsley
lemon wedges
salt and pepper

IMPERIAL
trout
large nub of butter per fish
$\frac{1}{2}$ oz coarse oatmeal per fish
parsley
lemon wedges
salt and pepper

Clean the trout. Cut open and remove the backbone. Melt the fat in a frying pan. Season the oatmeal and roll the fish in it. Fry the fish in the butter until golden brown on both sides. Drain on kitchen paper. Serve garnished with parsley and lemon wedges.

SWEET AND SOUR SALMON

METRIC
Marinade
Grated peel and juice from 1 lemon
2 tablespoons clear honey
2 tablespoons white wine vinegar
2 tablespoons soy sauce
2 tablespoons Worcester sauce
1 tablespoon sesame oil
Fish
4 Scottish salmon tail fillets (150 g each)

IMPERIAL
Marinade
Grated peel and juice from 1 lemon
2 tablespoons clear honey
2 tablespoons white wine vinegar
2 tablespoons soy sauce
2 tablespoons Worcester sauce
1 tablespoon sesame oil
Fish
4 Scottish salmon tail fillets (6 oz each)

Marinade: In a saucepan, combine all the marinade ingredients and simmer for 7 minutes to reduce a little. Allow to cool.

Fish: Place salmon fillets on a tray and pour the marinade on top. Cover with cling film and leave for 2-3 hours in a fridge. Remove from marinade and barbecue or grill for a total of 4 minutes or until cooked, turning once. Serve with new potatoes and mixed salad.

BARBECUE SALMON

METRIC	*IMPERIAL*
cubes of Scottish salmon	*cubes of Scottish salmon*
diced pineapple	*diced pineapple*
shallots	*shallots*
cherry tomatoes	*cherry tomatoes*
lemon	*lemon*
olive oil	*olive oil*
salt and pepper	*salt and pepper*

Alternate cubes of salmon on wooden skewers with diced pineapple, shallots, cherry tomatoes and slices of lemon. Brush with olive oil and season with salt and pepper. Cook for 2 minutes on each side. NB. Soaking the wooden skewers in cold water prior to filling prevents them from charring too quickly.

LEMON THYME BARBECUE SALMON

METRIC	*IMPERIAL*
bunch of lemon thyme	*bunch of lemon thyme*
4 Scottish salmon steaks (150 g each)	*4 Scottish salmon steaks (6 oz each)*
olive oil	*olive oil*
salt and pepper	*salt and pepper*

Lay out the thyme on the embers to allow the fragrance to waft over the salmon as it is cooking. Brush the salmon steaks lightly with oil. Season and barbecue for 4 minutes or until cooked, turning once. Serve with new potatoes and hollandaise sauce.

ROLLED HERRINGS

METRIC	IMPERIAL
6 herrings	6 herrings
vinegar	vinegar
water	water
2 bay leaves	2 bay leaves
10 peppercorns	10 peppercorns
salt and pepper	salt and pepper

Bone the herrings. Roll up the fish with the skins outside and place in a fireproof dish. Mix equal parts of vinegar and water and add enough to cover halfway up the fish. Add the bay leaves, seasoning and peppercorns. Cover and bake in a moderate oven (180°C, 350°F, gas mark 4) for 45 minutes.

KIPPER PATE

METRIC	IMPERIAL
125 g kipper fillets	5 oz kipper fillets
2 tablespoons white wine	2 tablespoons white wine
25 g butter	1 oz butter
25 g cream cheese	1 oz cream cheese
black pepper	black pepper

Poach the fish in water to remove some of the salt. Skin the fish and remove the bones. Cover with the wine and leave to marinate overnight. Remove the fish. Mash the fish with the other ingredients until smooth. Place the pâté in small jars. Chill. Serve with fingers of toast.

CREAMED HADDIES

METRIC	IMPERIAL
Sauce	**Sauce**
25 g butter	1 oz butter
25 g flour	1 oz flour
250 ml milk	$\frac{1}{2}$ pint milk
salt and pepper	salt and pepper
Fish	**Fish**
200 g haddock	8 oz haddock
50 g mushrooms	2 oz mushrooms
1 tomato	1 tomato
1 tablespoon grated cheese	1 tablespoon grated cheese
12 g butter.	$\frac{1}{2}$ oz butter

Sauce: Melt the butter and work in the flour using a wooden spoon. Add the milk slowly, stirring all the time to prevent lumps forming. Heat gently for 3 minutes.

Fish: Fillet the fish and slice the mushrooms and tomato. Place the fish fillets in a fireproof dish and add the mushrooms and tomato. Cover with the white sauce. Sprinkle with the grated cheese and dot with the butter. Bake in a moderate oven (190°C, 375°F, gas mark 5) for 20 minutes until brown.

TATTIES AN' HERRIN'

METRIC	IMPERIAL
potatoes, herrings, salt	potatoes, herrings, salt

Peel the potatoes or scrub them well. Place in a large saucepan. Cover with water. Season and bring to the boil. Wash and clean the herrings. When the potatoes are half cooked, pour away most of the water. Place the herrings over the potatoes. Put the lid on the saucepan and heat very gently so that the potatoes and fish cook in the steam from the remaining water.

MEAT

POACHER'S CASSEROLE

METRIC
1 rabbit
1 onion
1 carrot
4 rashers bacon
100 g peas
½ teaspoon mixed herbs
500 ml stock
salt and pepper

IMPERIAL
1 rabbit
1 onion
1 carrot
4 rashers bacon
4 oz peas
½ teaspoon mixed herbs
1 pint stock
salt and pepper

Skin, clean and joint the rabbit. Skin and thinly slice the onion. Peel and slice the carrot. Cover the bottom of a pie dish with rabbit meat. Place two rashers of bacon on top and then cover with half the vegetables and herbs. Season. Add the rest of the meat and the remaining vegetables and herbs. Put the remaining bacon on top. Season. Pour the stock over the mixture. Cook in a moderately hot oven (190ºC, 375ºF, gas mark 5) for 1½ hours for a young rabbit or 2½ hours for an older rabbit.

ROAST GAME

METRIC	IMPERIAL
2 birds	2 birds
4 rashers of fatty bacon	4 rashers of fatty bacon
2 rounds of bread	2 rounds of bread
50 g butter	2 oz butter
flour	flour
2 croutes of toast	2 croutes of toast
salt and pepper	salt and pepper
Gravy	*Gravy*
giblets	giblets
1 dessertspoon flour	1 dessertspoon flour
sediment in roasting tin	sediment in roasting tin

Game: Wash and dry the birds, use the giblets for stock. Put a nub of seasoned butter inside each bird. Truss. Cover the breasts with the bacon and place on the bread in a roasting tin. Melt the butter and spoon over the birds. Bake in the centre of a very hot oven (230ºC, 450ºF, gas mark 8) for 10 minutes then in a slightly cooler oven (204°C, 400ºF, gas mark 6) for a further 20-30 minutes. Baste frequently. 5 minutes before the end of the cooking time, froth the breasts to crisp the skin. This is done by removing the bacon, basting the breasts and dredging with flour. Return to a very hot oven (230ºC, 450ºF, gas mark 8) until brown and frothy. Serve on croutes of toast with clear, thin gravy, bread sauce (see next page), game chips and a green salad.

Gravy: Wash the giblets and remove any fat. Check that the greenish gall bladder is also removed. Cover the giblets with cold water. Season and simmer for 1 hour until tender. Pour off the fat from the meat tin and work 1 dessertspoonful of flour into the sediment. Strain the giblet stock and add to the roasting tin. Mix well and season. Add browning if necessary and bring to the boil.

BREAD SAUCE

METRIC
1 medium-sized onion
2 cloves
450 ml milk
75 g white breadcrumbs
25 g butter
salt and pepper

IMPERIAL
1 medium-sized onion
2 cloves
$\frac{3}{4}$ pint milk
3 oz white breadcrumbs
1 oz butter
salt and pepper

Skin the onion and press the cloves into it. Place in a saucepan with the milk and breadcrumbs. Season. Cover and leave to stand in a warm place for 1 hour. Simmer gently for 5 minutes taking care not to burn the sauce. Remove the onion and stir in the butter. Keep hot in a covered dish.

A STOVED HOWTOWDIE WI'DRAPPIT EGGS

METRIC
Stuffing
50 g breadcrumbs
2 tablespoons milk
1 small shallot - finely chopped
1 teaspoon chopped tarragon
1 teaspoon chopped parsley
salt and pepper

IMPERIAL
Stuffing
2 oz breadcrumbs
2 tablespoons milk
1 small shallot - finely chopped
1 teaspoon chopped tarragon
1 teaspoon chopped parsley
salt and pepper

Bird
2 kg roasting chicken
100 g butter
6 small onions or shallots
2 cloves
4 black peppercorns
pinch mace
salt and pepper
600 ml stock - from giblets
I kg spinach
4 eggs
small piece liver
2 tablespoons cream

Bird
3-4 lb roasting chicken
4 oz butter
6 small onions or shallots
2 cloves
4 black peppercorns
pinch mace
salt and pepper
1 pint stock - from giblets
2 lb spinach
4 eggs
small piece liver
2 tablespoons cream

Stuffing: Moisten the breadcrumbs with milk and add the chopped shallot, tarragon and parsley. Season and mix.
Bird: Wash and clean the bird. Put the stuffing in the bird. Melt half the butter in a casserole and lightly brown the onions. Place the bird in the middle of the dish and cook for 20 minutes in a hot oven (200ºC, 400ºF, gas mark 6). Add the herbs, seasoning and stock. Cover and cook for $1\frac{1}{2}$ hours at 180ºC, 350ºF, gas mark 4 until the bird is tender. Cook the spinach separately, drain and keep hot. Remove the bird on to a hot platter and pour the stock into a saucepan. Poach 4 eggs in this stock. Place the spinach around the chicken and place the eggs on the spinach. Chop the liver and add to the stock. Simmer for 5-10 minutes. Mash the liver to thicken the stock. Remove from the heat and add the cream and remaining butter cut into small pieces. Re-heat but do not boil. Pour the sauce over the chicken but not over the spinach.

BRAISED VENISON

METRIC
Marinade
125 ml red wine
1 tablespoon olive oil
1 onion
1 bay leaf
4 black peppercorns
Game
1 kg haunch of venison
25 g dripping
1 onion
1 orange
1 medium-sized carrot
4 sticks celery
250 ml stock
1 teaspoon salt
1 tablespoon redcurrant jelly
15 g flour
15g butter

IMPERIAL
Marinade
$\frac{1}{4}$ pint red wine
1 tablespoon olive oil
1 onion
1 bay leaf
4 black peppercorns
Game
2 lb haunch of venison
1 oz dripping
1 onion
1 orange
1 medium-sized carrot
4 sticks celery
$\frac{1}{2}$ pint stock
1 teaspoon salt
1 tablespoon redcurrant jelly
$\frac{1}{2}$ oz flour
$\frac{1}{2}$ oz butter

Marinade: Put all the ingredients of the marinade into a large pan and bring to the boil. Cool. Wash the venison and place in a large dish. Cover with the cold marinade. Leave for 24 hours, turning the meat occasionally. Drain and dry.
Game: Melt the dripping in an ovenproof dish and brown the meat on all sides. Remove from the dish. Skin and dice the onion. Peel the orange. Peel and dice the carrot. Cut up the celery. Place the prepared vegetables, with strips of

orange peel, in the dish. Cover and cook gently for 5-10 minutes until the onion is soft. Strain the marinade liquor into the dish and add the stock. Place the venison on top of the vegetables. Season. Cover and cook slowly for $2\frac{1}{2}$ hours until the meat is tender. Remove the meat and vegetables and keep hot in a large dish. Decant the liquor into a pan, add the orange juice and redcurrant jelly. Work the flour into the butter. Bring the liquid in the pan to the boil and add the butter/flour in small pieces to thicken it.

GILLIES VENISON

METRIC
1 kg venison
seasoned flour
50 g bacon fat
1 onion
2 rashers streaky bacon
50 g flour
600 ml stock
2 tablespoons port wine
salt and pepper

IMPERIAL
2 lb venison
seasoned flour
2 oz bacon fat
1 onion
2 rashers streaky bacon
2 oz g flour
1 pint stock
2 tablespoons port wine
salt and pepper

Cut the meat into 2•5 cm (1 inch) cubes and dip in seasoned flour. Melt the fat in a casserole dish. Skin and slice the onion and heat gently in the fat until it begins to colour. Add the pieces of venison and turn gently until they brown. Chop the bacon and add to the casserole. Season. Cover and cook for 1 hour until the meat is tender. Drain the meat on to absorbent kitchen paper. Decant excess fat from the pan. Stir the flour into the remaining sediment. Stir in the stock and pour in the port wine. Serve with mashed potatoes and green vegetables.

WILD DUCK AND PORT WINE SAUCE

METRIC
wild duck
salt and pepper
Sauce
I tablespoon red currant jelly
4 tablespoons port wine
300 ml game or mutton stock

IMPERIAL
wild duck
salt and pepper
Sauce
I tablespoon red currant jelly
4 tablespoons port wine
$\frac{1}{2}$ pint game or mutton stock

Clean the duck. Wipe inside and out. Brush with a little oil and sprinkle with salt and pepper. Prick the skin to release fat during cooking. Roast in the centre of the oven at 190ºC, 375ºF, gas mark 5, allowing 20 minutes per 400 g (per lb). Move to the top of the oven and roast for a further 10 minutes at 220°C, 425ºF, gas mark 7. Serve with port wine sauce, orange salad and game chips.

Sauce: Gently warm all the ingredients together in a saucepan until the jelly has dissolved.

GAME CHIPS

METRIC
potatoes
fat

IMPERIAL
potatoes
fat

Peel the potatoes and slice very thinly. Leave to stand in cold water for 1 hour. Drain and dry thoroughly. Fry in hot deep fat until golden brown. Stir with a metal spoon to prevent them from sticking together. Remove from the fat and drain well.

ORANGE SALAD

METRIC
Dressing
1 onion
1 tablespoon salad oil
pinch cayenne pepper
pinch salt and pepper
1 tablespoon lemon juice
1 tablespoon vinegar
Salad
oranges
sugar

IMPERIAL
Dressing
1 onion
1 tablespoon salad oil
pinch cayenne pepper
pinch salt and pepper
1 tablespoon lemon juice
1 tablespoon vinegar
Salad
oranges
sugar

Dressing: Rub a small bowl with the cut onion. Mix the oil and seasonings together. Gradually add the lemon juice and vinegar, stirring well. Beat.
Salad: Peel and thinly slice the oranges. Place in a salad dish sprinkling the slices with sugar. Pour the dressing over the fruit and keep very cold until served.

CASSEROLE GAME

METRIC
Marinade
3 shallots
125 ml Burgundy
1 tablespoon salad oil
4 black peppercorns
sprig of fresh thyme and marjoram
2 bay leaves
slice of lemon
Game
2 birds
6 small onions
25 g butter
2 tablespoons sugar
50 g button mushrooms
1 tablespoon flour
salt and pepper

IMPERIAL
Marinade
3 shallots
$\frac{1}{4}$ pint Burgundy
1 tablespoon salad oil
4 black peppercorns
sprig of fresh thyme and marjoram
2 bay leaves
slice of lemon
Game
2 birds
6 small onions
1 oz butter
2 tablespoons sugar
2 oz button mushrooms
1 tablespoon flour
salt and pepper

Marinade: Slice the shallots and place all the ingredients for the marinade in an enamelled pan and bring to the boil. Cool. Wash and dry the birds. Truss. Pour the cold marinade over the birds and leave to soak overnight turning once or twice.

Game: Skin the onions and boil in salted water until tender. Drain. Melt half of the butter and add with the sugar to the onion. Stir and cook until the onions begin to colour. Place the birds and the onions in an ovenproof dish. Melt the remaining butter in a pan and sauté the mushroom caps. Add to the casserole. Work the flour into the juices in the pan and gradually stir in the wine marinade. Season to taste and simmer gently to thicken. Strain over the birds. Add the mushroom stalks. Cover and cook in the centre of a moderate oven (180ºC, 350ºF, gas mark 4) for 1 hour until the birds are tender. Serve with jacket potatoes, green salad and rowan jelly.

SAVOURIES
POT HAGGIS

METRIC

200 g liver
1 medium-sized onion
75 g coarse oatmeal
50 g beef suet
300 ml beef stock
salt and pepper

IMPERIAL

8 oz liver
1 medium-sized onion
3 oz coarse oatmeal
2 oz beef suet
$\frac{1}{2}$ pint beef stock
salt and pepper

Cut up the liver. Skin and slice the onion. Simmer in salted water for 30-40 minutes until the meat is tender. When cool, mince the meat. Heat the oatmeal gently in a thick frying pan until it browns. Shred the suet. Mix the suet, meat, onion and oatmeal together. Add enough liquor from the meat to give the mixture a soft dropping consistency. Season to taste. Place in a greased pudding basin and close with foil. Steam for 2 hours. Serve with mashed potatoes and turnips.

HIGHLAND BEEF BALLS

METRIC

400 g beef steak
200 g suet
$\frac{1}{2}$ teaspoon saltpetre
$\frac{1}{2}$ teaspoon sugar
$\frac{1}{2}$ teaspoon ground ginger
$\frac{1}{4}$ teaspoon ground cloves
fat for frying
salt and black pepper

IMPERIAL

1 lb beef steak
$\frac{1}{2}$ lb suet
$\frac{1}{2}$ teaspoon saltpetre
$\frac{1}{2}$ teaspoon sugar
$\frac{1}{2}$ teaspoon ground ginger
$\frac{1}{4}$ teaspoon ground cloves
fat for frying
salt and black pepper

Mince the beef steak and suet. Mix all the ingredients together, except a little of the suet. Melt the suet kept back. Form the meat mixture into small balls and cover with a little melted suet. Fry in deep fat.

SKIRLIE

METRIC
50 g dripping or suet
1 onion
100 g oatmeal
salt and pepper

IMPERIAL
2 oz dripping or suet
1 onion
4 oz oatmeal
salt and pepper

Melt the fat. Skin and dice the onion and fry lightly in the fat. Stir in the oatmeal to make a thick mixture. Season to taste and cook for a few minutes. Serve hot with mashed potatoes, turnips or boiled potatoes.

MINCE COLLOPS

METRIC
1 medium-sized onion
400 g steak
25 g suet
15 g cooking fat
25 g oatmeal
250 ml beef stock
dash of mushroom ketchup or Worcester sauce
salt and pepper

IMPERIAL
1 medium-sized onion
1 lb steak
1 oz suet
$\frac{1}{2}$ oz cooking fat
1 oz oatmeal
$\frac{1}{2}$ pint beef stock
dash of mushroom ketchup or Worcester sauce
salt and pepper

Melt the fat in a frying pan. Skin and cut up the onion. Fry the onion gently until it starts to colour. Mince the steak and shred the suet. Add to the pan. Stir with a wooden spoon to separate the pieces of meat. Heat until the meat until the meat begins to brown. Stir in the oatmeal and enough stock to just cover the meat mixture. Season and flavour to taste, adding mushroom ketchup or Worcester sauce if liked. Simmer for 45 minutes to 1 hour. Serve on toast topped by poached eggs.

HIGHLAND CRUDDY BUTTER OR CROWDIE

METRIC
1 litre fresh or sour milk
½ teaspoon rennet
1 tablespoon cream
salt and pepper

IMPERIAL
2 pints fresh or sour milk
½ teaspoon rennet
1 tablespoon cream
salt and pepper

Gently warm the milk until it is tepid. Stir in the rennet and leave to stand in a warm place until a curd is formed. Cut into 2•5 cm (1 inch) cubes and leave to stand for 10 minutes for the whey to separate. Run off as much whey as possible and tie the curds in muslin. When dry, stir in the cream and season to taste. Pack into a mould. Herbs, chopped almonds or walnuts may also be added.

INKY-PINKY

METRIC
15 g beef fat
1 onion
25 g flour
beef stock
cold roast beef
boiled carrots
salt and pepper

IMPERIAL
½ oz beef fat
1 onion
1 oz flour
beef stock
cold roast beef
boiled carrots
salt and pepper

Melt the fat in a pan. Skin and slice the onion. Heat gently in the pan until it begins to colour. Remove the onion and work in the flour using a wooden spoon. Stir in the stock to make a brown gravy. Slice the beef and carrots and place in a deep pan with the onion. Cover with the gravy and simmer until heated thoroughly. Season to taste. Serve hot with boiled potatoes.

COLCANNON

METRIC	IMPERIAL
1 medium-sized cabbage	*1 medium-sized cabbage*
400 g potatoes	*1 lb potatoes*
400 g turnips	*1 lb turnips*
400 g carrots	*1 lb carrots*
15 g butter	*$\frac{1}{2}$ oz butter*
brown sauce	*brown sauce*
salt and pepper	*salt and pepper*

Clean and boil the cabbage in salted water. Boil the potatoes, turnips and carrots in salted water. Drain the cabbage and shred finely. Drain the vegetables and mash. Melt the butter in a pan and add all the vegetables. Mix together. Season to taste and add a little brown sauce. Serve hot with cold meats.

SCOTCH EGGS

METRIC	IMPERIAL
5 eggs	*5 eggs*
1 tablespoon flour	*1 tablespoon flour*
1 teaspoon mixed herbs	*1 teaspoon mixed herbs*
1 tablespoon finely chopped parsley	*1 tablespoon finely chopped parsley*
200 g pork sausage meat	*8 oz pork sausage meat*
50 g browned breadcrumbs	*2 oz browned breadcrumbs*
fat for frying	*fat for frying*
salt and pepper	*salt and pepper*

Hard boil 4 of the eggs for 10 minutes. Pour off the hot water and fill the pan with cold water. When they are cooled, shell the eggs. Season the flour and dust the eggs with it. Mix the herbs and parsley into the sausage meat and divide it into four. Cover each egg with sausage meat. Lightly beat the uncooked egg. Brush the Scotch eggs with the beaten egg and roll in breadcrumbs. Fry the eggs in deep fat turning occasionally until golden brown. Drain on absorbent kitchen paper.

COLLOPS IN THE PAN

METRIC
2 onions
butter for frying
4 slices rump or fillet steak
2 teaspoons oyster or walnut pickle
salt and pepper

IMPERIAL
2 onions
butter for frying
4 slices rump or fillet steak
2 teaspoons oyster or walnut pickle
salt and pepper

Skin and slice the onions. Melt the butter in a frying pan and add the onions. Heat until the onions are softened but not coloured. Push them to one side and put the steak in the pan. Brown and seal quickly on both sides. Arrange the onions around the meat. Season. Cover and cook quickly for 10 minutes. When cooked, place the steaks on a warm platter. Stir the oyster or walnut pickle into the pan. Bring to the boil, heat for 1 minute and pour over the steaks. Serve with jacket potatoes and green vegetables.

MUTTON PIES

METRIC	IMPERIAL
300 g lean mutton	12 oz lean mutton
1 small minced onion or shallot	1 small minced onion or shallot
$\frac{1}{2}$ teaspoon ground mace or nutmeg	$\frac{1}{2}$ teaspoon ground mace or nutmeg
1 teaspoon Worcester sauce	1 teaspoon Worcester sauce
or mushroom ketchup	or mushroom ketchup
4 tablespoons beef stock or water	4 tablespoons beef stock or water
hotwater pastry (see below)	hotwater pastry (see below)
egg or milk to glaze	egg or milk to glaze

Remove any skin or bone from the meat. Cut the meat into small pieces. Mix all the ingredients together, moistened with the beef stock. Roll out and cut six circles of hotwater pastry using a tumbler. Line six patty tins. Fill each tin with the meat mixture. Cut six lids from the remaining pastry. Moisten the edges of the pastry cases and close with the lids. Brush with beaten egg or milk. Make a hole in each. Cook for 15 minutes in a hot oven (220°C, 425°F gas mark 7) for 15 minutes until the pastry is brown. Cook for a further 20 minutes in a moderate oven (180°C 350°F, gas mark 4) until the meat is cooked.

HOTWATER PASTRY

METRIC	IMPERIAL
100 g beef dripping	4 oz beef dripping
250 ml water	$\frac{1}{2}$ pint water
400 g flour	1 lb flour
$\frac{1}{2}$ teaspoon salt	$\frac{1}{2}$ teaspoon salt

Gently heat the dripping with the water until it boils. Sift flour and salt together and put into a basin. Make a hole in the centre. Pour the dripping/water mixture into the flour and work in quickly with a knife. When cool enough to handle form into a lump and turn out on to a floured board. Knead lightly. Roll out and use.

CAKES AND BISCUITS
PETTICOAT TAILS

METRIC	IMPERIAL
2 teaspoons caraway seeds (optional)	*2 teaspoons caraway seeds (optional)*
300 g flour	*12 oz flour*
150 g butter	*6 oz butter*
150 ml milk	*$\frac{1}{4}$ pint milk*
40 g caster suger	*$1\frac{1}{2}$ oz caster sugar*

Mix the caraway seeds, if used, with the flour. Melt the butter in the milk. Make a hole in the middle of the flour and pour the butter/milk into it. Knead lightly until the mixture comes together. Turn on to a lightly floured board and roll out to a thicknes of 0•75 cm ($\frac{1}{4}$ inch) . Lay an inverted dinner plate on top and cut out a large circle. Remove the plate. Place a tumbler in the centre of the circle of paste and cut out a small circle. Keep the smaller circle whole but cut the outer part into segments or tails. Do not cut right through the paste. Bake on a greased baking tray in a moderate oven (180ºC, 350ºF, gas mark 4) for 20 minutes until crisp and golden. Cool on a wire rack and dust with caster sugar.

RAISIN SHORTBREAD

METRIC	IMPERIAL
100 g butter	*4 oz butter*
50 g caster sugar	*2 oz caster sugar*
200 g flour	*8 oz flour*
100 g raisins	*4 oz raisins*

Cream the butter and sugar together. Work in the flour to make a firm dough. Divide in half. Roll out each piece into a rectangle of 0•75 cm thickness ($\frac{1}{4}$ inch). Spread the raisins over one piece and place the other piece on top. Press together and pinch the edges. Prick well. Bake for 45 minutes at 180ºC, 350ºF, gas mark 4. Cut into pieces when cool.

DUNDEE CAKE

METRIC

150 g butter
150 g caster sugar
4 eggs
2 tablespoons ground almonds
150 g currants
150 g sultanas
50 g glacé cherries
50 g mixed peel
grated rind and juice of half lemon
200 g flour
1 teaspoon baking powder
pinch salt
1 tablespoon brandy or rum
25 g blanched almonds for top of cake

Glaze

2 tablespoons milk
1 tablespoon sugar

IMPERIAL

6 oz butter
6 oz caster sugar
4 eggs
2 tablespoons ground almonds
6 oz currants
6 oz sultanas
2 oz glacé cherries
2 oz mixed peel
grated rind and juice of half lemon
8 oz flour
1 teaspoon baking powder
pinch salt
1 tablespoon brandy or rum
1 oz blanched almonds for top of cake

Glaze

2 tablespoons milk
1 tablespoon sugar

Grease an 8-inch round cake tin and line with greased greaseproof paper. Prepare the fruit. Cream the butter and sugar together until the mixture is white and fluffy. Beat in the eggs, one at a time, adding a little flour to prevent curdling. Stir in the ground almonds, fruit, mixed peel, grated lemon rind and lemon juice. Sift the flour, baking powder and pinch of salt together. Fold into the cake mixture. Stir in the brandy or rum. Turn into the cake tin. Cover with foil and bake in a moderate oven (150°C, 300°F, gas mark 2) for about $2\frac{1}{2}$ hours. Half way through the cooking time, remove the foil and scatter the almonds on top. When the cake is cooked, a skewer or needle inserted into the cake comes out clean.

To glaze: When the cake is nearly cooked, dissolve the tablespoon of sugar in the milk and brush the top of the cake. Allow the cake to cool in the tin. If preferred, the rum or brandy may be poured over the base of the cake after it is cooked. The cake may be kept for months in a tin. [There is an alternative recipe for Dundee Cake in *Scottish Teas*}

BROONIE

METRIC	*IMPERIAL*
100 g flour	*4 oz flour*
1 teaspoon bicarbonate of soda	*1 teaspoon bicarbonate of soda*
1 teaspoon ground ginger	*1 teaspoon ground ginger*
125 g medium oatmeal	*5 oz medium oatmeal*
50 g butter	*2 oz butter*
2 tablespoons black treacle	*2 tablespoons black treacle*
75 g sugar	*3 oz sugar*
1 egg	*1 egg*
250 ml sour milk or buttermilk	*$\frac{1}{2}$ pint sour milk or buttermilk*

Sift the flour, bicarbonate of soda and ginger together. Add the oatmeal. Rub in the butter until the mixture looks like breadcrumbs. Melt the treacle. Stir into the flour mixture together with the sugar and egg. Add enough sour milk or buttermilk to make the mixture just soft enough to drop from a spoon. Turn into a greased tin and bake in a moderate oven (170°C, 325°F, gas mark 3) for 1-$\frac{1}{2}$ hours until firm and well risen. Cool on a wire tray.

AYRSHIRE SHORTBREAD

METRIC	IMPERIAL
100 g flour and 100 g ground rice or	*4 oz flour and 4 oz ground rice or*
175 g flour and 25 g cornflour	*7 oz flour and I oz cornflour*
100 g butter	*4 oz butter*
75 g caster sugar	*3 oz caster sugar*
1 egg yolk	*1 egg yolk*
1 teaspoon cream	*1 teaspoon cream*

Sieve the flours together and lightly rub in the butter. Stir in the sugar. Lightly beat the egg yolk. Bind the mixture together with the egg yolk and the cream. Turn on to a floured board. Divide in half and press out into two rounds. Lightly roll out the rounds to a thickness of half inch. Crimp the edges and mark each round into 6-8 sections. Prick with a fork and cook in the centre of a cool oven (150°C, 300°F, gas mark 2) for 45 minutes until firm and browned. Cool on a wire rack and dredge with caster sugar. Break into pieces. Alternatively, the mixure may be rolled into two rectangles and marked in strips.

OATMEAL BISCUITS

METRIC	IMPERIAL
150 g self-raisingflour	*6 oz self-raising flour*
150 g oatmeal	*6 oz oatmeal*
25 g sugar	*1 oz sugar*
75 g butter	*3 oz butter*
milk	*milk*
pinch of salt	*pinch of salt*

Mix the dry ingredients together and rub in the fat. Add enough milk to make a stiff mixture. Roll out thinly on a board lightly sprinkled with oatmeal. Cut into biscuits and prick all over. Bake on a greased baking sheet in a moderate oven (180°C, 350°F, gas mark 4) for 20 minutes.

EDINBURGH GINGERBREAD

METRIC
400 g flour
1 teaspoon baking powder
$\frac{1}{4}$ teaspoon salt
1 teaspoon ground ginger
1 teaspoon cinnamon
1 teaspoon mixed spice
$\frac{1}{2}$ teaspoon ground cloves
200 g dates
100 g walnuts
150 g black treacle
200 g brown sugar
150 g butter
2 eggs
150 ml milk
preserved ginger

IMPERIAL
1 Ib flour
1 teaspoon baking powder
$\frac{1}{4}$ teaspoon salt
1 teaspoon ground ginger
1 teaspoon cinnamon
1 teaspoon mixed spice
$\frac{1}{2}$ teaspoon ground cloves
8 oz dates
4 oz walnuts
6 oz black treacle
8 oz brown sugar
6 oz butter
2 eggs
$\frac{1}{4}$ pint milk
preserved ginger

Grease a 7-inch square tin and line with greased greaseproof paper. Sift the flour, baking powder, salt and spices together. Stone and chop the dates. Shell and chop the walnuts. Add the dates and walnuts to the flour mixture. Warm the treacle, sugar and butter together. Whisk the eggs lightly. Add the treacle mixture and the eggs to the flour mixture. Add enough milk to give a dropping consistency. The mixture should not be too soft. Pour into the tin and bake in a moderate oven (180°C, 350°F, gas mark 4) for $1\frac{1}{2}$ hours until the gingerbread is firm to the touch. Cool on a wire rack. Cut into squares and decorate with pieces of preserved ginger.

BANNOCK OR OATCAKE

METRIC	IMPERIAL
100 g oatmeal	4 oz oatmeal
pinch bicarbonate soda	pinch bicarbonate soda
pinch salt	pinch salt
1 teaspoon bacon fat	1 teaspoon bacon fat
2 tablespoons warm water	2 tablespoons warm water

Mix the oatmeal, bicarbonate of soda and salt together. Make a well in the middle of the mixture and pour in the melted fat. Add enough water to make a stiff dough. Turn out on a board liberally scattered with oatmeal. Knead lightly and then roll out to a thickness of 0*5 cm ($\frac{1}{4}$ inch). Keep the dough well dusted with oatmeal to stop it sticking. Form into a round using a plate. Sprinkle again with oatmeal and cook on a warmed girdle until the edges begin to curl. Turn and cook the other side. The bannock may be cut into quarters or farls. Another bannock may be prepared while the first is cooking. Dough for more than one bannock cannot be prepared at the same time because the dough stiffens so quickly.

SWEET BANNOCKS

METRIC	IMPERIAL
175 g fine oatmeal	7 oz fine oatmeal
100 g self-raising flour	4 oz self-raising flour
100 g caster sugar	4 oz caster sugar
75 g butter	3 oz butter
4 tablespoons water	4 tablespoons water

Mix the dry ingredients together. Melt the butter with the water in a saucepan and pour into the centre of the oatmeal mixture. Mix well. Turn on to a floured board and roll out to a thickness of 0•75 cm ($\frac{1}{4}$ inch). Cut into rounds and bake at 200ºC. 400ºF, gas mark 6 for 15 minutes. Turn off the oven and leave to cool in the oven. Serve with jam and cream.

PUDDINGS AND DESSERTS

BUTTERSCOTCH PIE

METRIC	IMPERIAL
Shortcrust pastry	*Shortcrust pastry*
50 g butter	2 oz butter
100 g plain flour	4 oz plain flour
2 tablespoons cold water	2 tablespoons cold water
Filling	*Filling*
75 g brown sugar	3 oz brown sugar
25 g flour	1 oz flour
3 tablespoons water	3 tablespoons water
125 ml milk	$\frac{1}{4}$ pint milk
25 g butter	1 oz butter
1 teaspoon vanilla essence	1 teaspoon vanilla essence
1 egg yolk	1 egg yolk
Meringue	*Meringue*
50 g caster sugar	2 oz caster sugar
1 egg white	1 egg white

Pastry Rub the butter into the flour until the mixture looks like breadcrumbs. Add the water and form into a ball. Roll out the pastry and line a flan tin. Bake blind.

Filling Mix the sugar and flour together and blend with the water. Heat the milk and pour over the mixture. Add the butter and mix well. Warm slowly until thick. Remove from the heat and add the flavouring. Add egg yolk to the mixture. Pour into the pastry case.

Meringue Whisk the egg white until stiff and fold in the caster sugar. Pile the meringue on top of the pie and bake in a cool oven (150ºC, 300ºF, gas mark 2) until browned.

DRAMBUIE CREAM TRIFLE

METRIC	*IMPERIAL*
1 orange jelly	*1 orange jelly*
sponge fingers or ratafia biscuits	*sponge fingers or ratafia biscuits*
400 ml milk	*¾ pints milk*
2 eggs	*2 eggs*
75 g caster sugar	*3 oz caster sugar*
20 g powdered gelatine	*¾ oz powdered gelatine*
250 ml cream	*½ pint cream*
2 - 3 tablespoons Drambuie	*2 - 3 tablespoons Drambuie*

Dissolve the jelly in hot water to make 600 ml solution (1 pint). Pour into a mould. When cool and thickened, but not set, line the sides of the mould with sponge fingers or ratafia biscuits. Leave to set. Bring the milk to the boil. Beat the eggs and blend with the sugar and gelatine. Pour the milk into the egg mixture and return to the saucepan. Heat gently for 3 minutes, stirring all the time. Do not boil. Whip the cream and add the Drambuie. When the egg custard is cool, but not set, fold in the cream mixture. Pour into the sponge finger lined mould and leave to set in a cool place.

PLUM PUDDING

METRIC	*IMPERIAL*
150 g raisins	*6 oz raisins*
150 g currants	*6 oz currants*
75 g chopped mixed peel	*3 oz chopped mixed peel*
150 g suet	*6 oz suet*

150 g flour
150 g breadcrumbs
150 g sugar
1 teaspoon baking powder
½ teaspoon salt
½ teaspoon ground mace
½ teaspoon grated nutmeg
2 eggs
1 tablespoon brandy
250 ml milk

Brandy Sauce
2 teaspoons cornflour
300 ml milk
15 g caster sugar
1 egg yolk
25 g butter
1 tablespoon brandy
1 tablespoon Madeira

6 oz flour
6 oz breadcrumbs
6 oz sugar
1 teaspoon baking powder
½ teaspoon salt
½ teaspoon ground mace
½ teaspoon grated nutmeg
2 eggs
1 tablespoon brandy
½ pint milk

Brandy Sauce
2 teaspoons cornflour
½ pint millk
½ oz caster sugar
1 egg yolk
1 oz butter
1 tablespoon brandy
1 tablespoon Madeira

Pudding: Wash, dry and stone the fruit. Finely shred the suet. Mix all the dry ingredients together. Lightly beat the eggs. Add the eggs and brandy with enough milk to bind the mixture together. Turn into a well greased basin and steam for 6-7 hours. Serve with brandy sauce.

Brandy Sauce: Make the cornflour into a smooth paste with a little of the milk. Heat the rest of the milk with the sugar and when boiling pour over the cornflour stirring all the time. Return the mixture to the saucepan and bring to the boil. Cook for 3 minutes until the mixture thickens, stirring to keep the sauce smooth. Remove from the heat and cool slightly. Beat the egg yolk and add with the butter, brandy and Madeira. Stir continuously over a low heat or in a double boiler. Do not let it boil or it will curdle. Pour over the pudding or serve separately.

PEACHES IN WHISKY

METRIC
8 fresh peaches
800 g caster sugar
500 ml water
3 tablespoons malt whisky
cream

IMPERIAL
8 fresh peaches
2 lb caster sugar
1 pint water
3 tablespoons malt whisky
cream

Soak the peaches for 5 minutes in water. Skin. Dissolve the sugar in 500 ml water (1 pint) and boil. Add the peaches and heat gently for 15 minutes. Remove the peaches. Add the whisky to the syrup and boil for 5 minutes. Cool and pour over the peaches. Chill. Serve with whipped cream.

CRANACHAN OR CREAM CROWDIE

METRIC
50 g pinhead oatmeal
250 ml double cream
25-50 g caster sugar
rum or vanilla essence
100 g raspberries

IMPERIAL
2 oz pinhead oatmeal
1 pint double cream
1-2 oz caster sugar
rum or vanilla essence
4 oz raspberries

Toast the oatmeal lightly in the oven or in a thick-bottomed frying pan over a gentle heat. Beat the cream until frothy but not stiff. Sweeten to taste. Mix in the oatmeal and flavour with rum or vanilla. Wash and sieve the raspberries and stir into the cream mixture.

SYLLABUB

METRIC
$\frac{1}{2}$ lemon
2 egg whites
100 g caster sugar
125 ml sweet white wine
275 ml double cream
crystallised lemon slices

IMPERIAL
$\frac{1}{2}$ lemon
2 egg whites
4 oz caster sugar
$\frac{1}{4}$ pint sweet white wine
$\frac{1}{2}$ pint double cream
crystallised lemon slices

Squeeze the lemon. Whisk the egg whites until stiff. Fold in the sugar, wine, lemon juice and cream. Pour into individual glasses and chill for several hours before serving. Decorate with lemon slices.

CALEDONIAN CREAM

METRIC
1 tablespoon Dundee orange marmalade
1 tablespoon sugar
1 tablespoon brandy or Highland unblended malt whisky
$\frac{1}{2}$ lemon
500 ml cream

IMPERIAL
1 tablespoon Dundee orange marmalade
1 tablespoon sugar
1 tablespoon brandy or Highland unblended malt whisky
$\frac{1}{2}$ lemon
1 pint cream

Add the marmalade, sugar, brandy or whisky and the juice of half a lemon to the cream. Whisk well. Turn into a mould and chill.

PRESERVES

DUNDEE MARMALADE

METRIC
1•5 kg Seville oranges
3 lemons
3 litres water
3 kg preserving or granulated sugar

IMPERIAL
3 lb Seville oranges
3 lemons
6 pints water
6 lb preserving or granulated sugar

Wash and scrub the fruit. Cut in half and squeeze out the juice. Tie the pips in a muslin bag. Slice the peel thinly. Cut up the orange halves and put into a large preserving pan with the water, the juice of the lemons, the bag of pips and sliced peel. Bring to the boil and heat gently until the peel is soft and the volume of the liquid is reduced by half. (About $1\frac{1}{2}$ hours.) Lift out the bag of pips, cool and squeeze dry over the pan. Add the sugar and stir until dissolved. Boil rapidly until setting point is reached (93-105°C, 200-222°F). Skim and pot in hot sterilized jars. Seal.

ROWAN JELLY

METRIC
1•5 kg rowan berries
500 g cooking apples
Granulated or loaf sugar

IMPERIAL
3 lb rowan berries
1 lb cooking apples
Granulated or loaf sugar

Wash the berries and remove the stalks. Drain. Wash the apples and cut them up, discarding the cores. Place the fruit in a preserving pan and add enough water to just cover the fruit. Simmer gently for 45 minutes. Strain through a jelly cloth. Measure the liquid as it is returned to the pan and allow 500 g sugar (1 lb) for each litre (2pints) of liquid. Stir until the mixture boils and all the sugar has dissolved. Continue heating until setting point is reached - about half an hour - when a drop of the liquid sets quickly on a cold plate. Skim and pour into sterilised jars and seal.

CONFECTIONERY
SCOTCH OATS

METRIC
100 g butter
150 g brown sugar
100 g rolled oats
$\frac{1}{2}$ teaspoon salt
1 teaspoon baking powder

IMPERIAL
4 oz butter
6 oz brown sugar
4 oz rolled oats
$\frac{1}{2}$ teaspoon salt
1 teaspoon baking powder

Warm the butter gently until it melts. Stir in the sugar. Add the rolled oats, salt and baking powder. Mix well. Turn into a greased 20cm (8 inch) square tin. Bake in a moderate oven (180ºC, 350ºF, gas mark 4) for 30 minutes. Leave to cool for a few minutes and then cut into squares. Remove from the tin before completely cooled.

WALNUT BITS

METRIC
200 g granulated sugar
25 g butter
3 tablespoons milk
2 teaspoons syrup
25 g chopped walnuts

IMPERIAL
8 oz granulated sugar
1 oz butter
3 tablespoons milk
2 teaspoons syrup
1 oz chopped walnuts

Mix the sugar, butter, milk and syrup together in a pan. Warm gently until the mixture boils and reaches the soft ball point (115ºC, 239ºF) stirring all the time. Remove from the heat and add the chopped walnuts. Beat until the mixture begins to grain. Pour into a greased tin 20 x 15 cm (8 x 6 inches). Break into pieces when cold. Dust with icing sugar and store in an airtight jar.

BUTTERSCOTCH

METRIC
400 g brown sugar
100 g butter
juice of 1 lemon or
1 teaspoon ground ginger

IMPERIAL
1 lb brown sugar
4 oz butter
juice of 1 lemon or
1 teaspoon ground ginger

Heat the sugar in a saucepan until it melts. Cream the butter and add slowly to the sugar. Continue heating and stirring until a little of the mixture hardens when dropped into cold water. Add the lemon juice or ground ginger. Beat quickly with a fork. Pour into a buttered tin and mark into squares. Break into pieces when cold.

TREACLE TOFFEE

METRIC
400 g demerara sugar
150 ml water
$\frac{1}{4}$ teaspoon cream of tartar
100 g black treacle
100 g golden syrup

IMPERIAL
1 lb demerara sugar
$\frac{1}{4}$ pint water
$\frac{1}{4}$ teaspoon cream of tartar
4 oz black treacle
4 oz golden syrup

Butter an 18-cm (7 inch) square tin. Pour the water into a heavy-based saucepan. Add the sugar. Warm over a low heat until the sugar has dissolved. Add the remaining ingredients and bring to the boil. Boil to the soft crack stage (132°C, 270°F). Pour into the tin and cool for 5 minutes. Mark into squares and leave to set.

DRINKS

TODDY

METRIC
whisky
sugar
hot water

IMPERIAL
whisky
sugar
hot water

Put 2 teaspoons sugar and a wine glass of hot water into a warmed tumbler. Stir until the sugar has dissolved. Add a wine glass of whisky and stir. Add another wine glass of hot water and a further wine glass of whisky.

SCOTTISH MILK

METRIC
2 eggs
50 g caster sugar
250 ml milk
4 tablespoons whisky
nutmeg

IMPERIAL
2 eggs
2 oz caster sugar
$\frac{1}{2}$ pint milk
4 tablespoons whisky
nutmeg

Separate the egg yolks and whites. Beat the egg yolks with the sugar until thick and creamy. Beat the milk and whisky into the egg yolk mixture. Add a little grated nutmeg. Beat the egg whites until stiff and fold into the milk mixture. Serve in chilled glasses.

INDEX